Praise for
The Psychic Power of Your Dreams: Practical Skills For Working With Your Dreams For Insight, Information, Creativity And A Better Life

"Catherine Kane has done it again. Her wit shines through a gentle introduction to the topic of dream interpretation. Haven't you had a dream that you'd like to find out what it meant? Sure, you have! And this book is a non-threatening and well presented discussion on the topic. Ms. Kane knows her topic; she is a top-flight palmist and empath, and I have had the good fortune to have attended a number of her workshops over the years. So if you're looking for some answers about dream work, here's your chance."

- Jane T. Sibley,
   Ph.D., traditional Norse practitioner
   and specialist in Norse folklore and runes.

"This book is about the self empowerment of dream work. The clear concise directions in this book allow the reader to better experience their own unique journey into the world of their dreams."

- Adam Latin,
   professional psychic

"Once again Catherine Kane has created a wonderfully accessible experience, like a visit with your fairy godmother with cocoa and cookies, wrapped up in an easy to read book. Have you been wondering if your dreams have something important to tell you? and if they do, how do you figure it out?

People have been writing dream interpretation books since the time of the Pharaohs, in Greece, Rome, and the Middle Ages, right up to the present, because humans spend a third of their lives dreaming, and the centuries have proven the value of paying attention to dreams. What makes this book especially valuable is that she recognizes that all dreams are not the same and cannot be read the same way. She describes many sorts of dreams and how you can work with them. (If your nightmare is from indigestion, better lay off the spicy snacks before bed!) How to tell the difference between literal and symbolic psychic dreams, and how to decipher your own personal symbol set (because your dreams don't use someone else's.) So this is not a book where you can look up crocodile, and read "If a man sees himself in a dream eating crocodile flesh it is good omen, meaning he will become a village official." (Yes, that's one of the Egyptian ones.)

Going beyond that, Cathy gives you lots of helpful hints (as any good fairy godmother would), about how to remember your dreams better, how to program your dreams, how to get the messages your dreams are trying to send; in short, she has a bit of something for everyone, delivered in a relaxed, friendly manner, that will make exploring these new skills easy and fun."

- Tchipakkan

Co-chair Changing Times, Changing Worlds conference
Metaphysical speaker, teacher and artist

And also for Catherine's previous books
Adventures in Palmistry

"The information in this book is clear, concise, hits the pertinent points of palmistry, and immediately lets you start practicing your craft."

-Adam Latin, professional palmist

"Ms. Kane is not only a talented palm reader, but a talented writer as well. She explains the concepts and techniques clearly, and with a sense of humor."

-Lois Fitzpatrick, leader, East Kingdom Soothsayer's guild,
    an organization studying
      the methods and history of psychic readings

The Practical Empath-
Surviving and Thriving as a Psychic Empath

"...Gives you a window of understanding as to who an empath is, a brief synopsis about energy and how it works, shielding techniques, how much input is too much, and so much more. Cathy is an amazing empath who has helped countless people to learn how to deal with this wonderful however sometimes daunting gift. This book makes a great read for the novice and the experienced empath alike. With Cathy's guidance, you will learn how to cope with being an empath and, hopefully, you will get as much, if not more, out of her book *The Practical Empath* as I did. Happy reading."

-Delilah Kieffer, spiritualist and psychic

Manifesting Something Better

"I have been privileged to attend Cathy's class on manifestation in the past and found her book on the subject to be the best of the in-person class and more. From basic concepts to different manifestation techniques and possible road blocks to success this book touches on everything you need to know in an easy to understand way. Whether you are new to manifestation or have some experience with it this book will provide you with the tools to take control of the energy you create in your own life."

- Morgan Daimler,
   author of *By Land, Sea, and Sky*
      and *A Child's Eye View of the Fairy Faith*

"Who doesn't want "what we want (when we want it)"? But how do we attract to ourselves a new job, better weather, a clearer vision, or the many other things that would make our lives better or easier? Catherine Kane leads us gently through the steps of Manifestation. She shows us how it works, how to avoid common ways we neutralize them, and makes it easy to believe that we can do it ourselves. She shares many different techniques, so that each of us can find something that will work for us. She does this all with humor and compassion, her genuine love for her readers coming through the pages, so that, when you are done with the book, you've not only got new skills for a better life, but a new friend."

- Tchipakkan
   -Co-chair Changing Times, Changing Worlds conference
      -Metaphysical speaker and artist
         -Host of "The New Normal" on liveparanormal.com

The Psychic Power of
Your Dreams:

**Practical Skills
For Working With Your Dreams
For Insight, Information, Creativity
And A Better Life**

By Catherine Kane

Also by Catherine Kane

Adventures in Palmistry

The Practical Empath-
Surviving and Thriving as a Psychic Empath

The Lands That Lie Between-
An Urban Fantasy with Morgan and Sam

Manifesting Something Better:
Easy Quick and Fun Ways to
Manifest the Life of Your Dreams

For more information,
please visit Foresight Publications
at www.ForesightYourPsychic.com

The Psychic Power of Your Dreams:

Practical Skills
For Working With Your Dreams
For Insight, Information, Creativity
And A Better Life

By Catherine Kane

The Psychic Power of Your Dreams: Practical Skills For Working With Your Dreams For Insight, Information, Creativity And A Better Life © October2013

By Catherine Kane

ISBN 978-0-9846951-2-6

Foresight Publications
Wallingford, CT.

This book is dedicated to

Jayee White Oak

Good friend and copy editor extraordinaire

Whose friendship,

unfailing good humor,

eagle eye for editing errors,

willingness to read genres she doesn't like,

ability to deal with unreasonable deadlines,

and amazing, amazing tact,

have made so many of my books better.

You help me do impossible things,

And this one's for you.

Acknowledgements

Here I am, zipping up the coat and kissing the forehead of my fifth book, and sending it out to play in the great, big, glorious world. Here's hoping it makes friends, helps people and makes this world a little better place.

As always, I haven't gotten to this place alone. There are a lot of you who have helped me get here and who deserve thanks- so here those thanks come…

To all of the teachers who taught me how to write, to think, to ask questions, to be creative and to become the person and writer I am today. The folks who think school only teaches you to conform sadly never met you guys.

Once again, to the wild and creative leaders and members of the Fairfield County Writer's group. You guys inspire the heck out of me.

To my readers and reviewers, Tchipakkan, Jane Sibley, Adam Latin, and Jayee White Oak. Your input helps me polish these words for all of my readers.

To my husband Starwolf, who's always got my back and supports me as a writer, a wife and a friend. I am so fortunate that we found each other.

To all of you who read my work, both old friends and new ones. Welcome to our journey together and I hope that you will find things you can use along the way.

And last but not least, to all of the dreamers. Dream big - and then wake up and bring your best dreams to life…

Table of Contents

Introduction

Do you dream?

Most of us do, whether we remember our dreams or not, and scientific studies find that dreams are an essential part of healthy sleep patterns.

But dreams are much more than that.

Dreams are a way to access our unconscious mind. Dreams can help us to get in touch with the beliefs we hold that create the world around us and how we connect with that world. Dreams are a way to gain insight and have the information we need to make better choices.

And dreams can put us in touch with our own natural psychic abilities.

Psychic? Who, us?

Yes.

We all seem to have senses beyond the basic five. We all seem to have ways of knowing things we cannot know through sight or sound or smell or taste or touch. We all have instincts and hunches and gut level reactions that are part of our own personal inner wisdom speaking to us.

And dreams are one of the ways in which that personal inner wisdom first surfaces in the lives of most people.

Dreams are your birth right- the very first tool that you receive for learning how to contact your inner wisdom. Would you like to learn how to use that tool?

That's what this book is about- teaching you practical skills for working with dreaming. How to remember your dreams. How to interpret your dreams. How to use your dreams to gather better information, become more creative, answer questions and resolve problems in your life.

That's all ahead of us now.

But first, I thought you might find it interesting to know how this book came to be written in the first place...

I like to write. I like to write a lot. I like to write magazine articles, and blog posts, and songs, and audience participation murder mystery games, and riddles, and poetry...

And books. I also like to write books.

And this is the beginning of my fifth one.

If you've read my books before, you may have noticed that most of my books fall within the category of "New Age" or "Occult". This book does too, of course.

You may have also noticed that most of my books and other writings are designed to teach you practical metaphysical skills for living in this magical world.

What you may not know is how I chose what I'm writing about...

As people go, I'm rather eclectic. I like to learn, and I've chased my curiosity into quite a number of different fields of knowledge either because they've directly applied to me or else because I've just gotten the feeling that a topic is one that I want to know more about. I've been active in the areas of spirituality, personal growth, metaphysics and alternative health for over 40 years, and, because I am a curious and delighted student of the Universe, have learned quite a number of different things in the process.

On top of that, I tend to lean towards the practical side of most of these topics. I like what I can work with. While I do enjoy the philosophy that goes with things esoteric, when push comes to shove, what I'm really interested in is your basic meat and potatoes metaphysics. I'm looking for the answers to questions like:

- How can I be healthier, or at least healthy enough to do the things I want to do?
- What kinds of things do I want to do with my life?
- How can energy work, or divination or magic or alternative health practices help me to do these things?
- What's the bottom line on how this metaphysics works, when we strip away all of the fancywindow dressing?
- What kinds of metaphysics would help me to reach my goals?
- If I have more than one choice, which one speaks to me more?
- How much time do I have to include these practices in my life?
- What am I willing to let go of from my present life to make these things happen? What am I not willing to let go of?
- Will I actually do the metaphysical activity I'm thinking of?
- How can magic help me make my life better?
- How can this help me? How can this help other people I come in contact with?

You know. Stuff like that. The nuts and bolts questions that help me to find the practical magic that will fit in a busy, happy life. The kind of magic that you may be looking for, too.

I don't have the time or the money to quit my job, dress all in white, strip my furniture down to a few throw pillows, and meditate for eight hours a day. I don't really **want** to quit my job, dress all in white, strip my furniture

3

down to a few throw pillows, and meditate for eight hours a day.

I'm your average middle aged woman who likes TV, and caffeine, and reading, and spending time with her friends, and fast food;

And magic. But I need the kind of magic that will fit into my funky, friendly, overly full but happy middle class life.

So that's what I look for.

And when I find it, I don't just make it part of my life. I also teach and write about it, because if this is practical magic for me, it may be practical for other folks as well.

And that brings us right to where we are now.

How do I choose what to write about?

I look at what I've learned that I've found useful to me and I write about that. I also look for the needs that are coming up for other people around me. I use those events as omens or indicators of something that needs to be addressed in the world.

I pretty much riff on what comes up. What's interesting to me is that, whenever I find myself ready to start writing about a new topic, suddenly someone with a new need will pop up, putting my new topic in front of me.

- "Adventures in Palmistry" started as an online course for a woman who wanted to learn palmistry, but was hundreds of miles away from where I lived.
- I wrote about scrying because I met a woman in a bookstore who had questions about it.
- "The Practical Empath" began because of everyempath that I met while doing readings who

4

needed to learn how to energetically shield and get better control of her gift.

- Folks trying to let go of the energy from emotional wounds of the past were the starting point for articles that I've written on grounding out negative energy.
- "Manifesting Something Better" came in response to a rush of people who'd heard about manifestation work in one of my classes or in an online comment, and who now wanted an   exhaustive   comment online   on   "everything   you   know   about manifestation"

You get the idea.
I write what I know.
And I write what people seem to need.
So why am I diving into dream work now?

It started slowly, as these things often do for me. I started running into people who'd talk about "that funny dream I had the other night" and wondering what it meant. One person, and then two, and then a steady stream of them - many different faces, but, over and over again, the same questions needing answers.

I started having people sit down at my table and ask me if they were going crazy because they were dreaming about things that would later on actually happen in their lives.

I found myself spending a lot of time talking to people about dreams. Explaining how they worked. Soothing folks and telling them that they weren't crazy when they felt that their dreams were telling them things. Getting them started on the basics of how to understand their own dreamings.

And then, in a period of less than 12 hours, while randomly reading a few blogs, I ran across posts by two totally unrelated people who were both very stressed by severely portentous dreams (One of a crash of the plane she was about to take, the other a recurring dream about setting up with the band before playing a performance...)

And, all at once, I felt the hair stand up on the back of my neck. It was time to write another book.

Dreams are the way that your inner wisdom first starts to speak to you. Classic dream manuals don't work (for reasons that we'll talk about in chapter 3.)

And people need the wisdom and the help that their dreams can bring them.

The signs around me are speaking. People have a need here, and so I'm going to Dreamland.

It's time to teach you the skills you to get the best out of your dreams.

To know where you're going, it helps to know where you've been. Let's start out our journey together with a look at the history of dream work.

Dreams and How They Work

Chapter 1
A Brief History of Dream Work

People have been working with dreams and with dream work for as long as there have been people. They've looked to dreams for information, for insight, for healing, for spiritual support and for a host of other benefits. Many cultures believed that dreams were one of the ways that the Divine Creator (whether god or goddess) communicated with man.

The Epic of Gilgamesh, written in the 18th century BC, is one of the earliest examples we have of dream interpretation. Gilgamesh dreamt of an axe that fell from the sky. His dream was interpreted by his mother, Ninsun, as information of the arrival of a rival who would then become Gilgamesh's greatest and most loyal ally.

Another record of dream interpretation in early times is that of Gudea, a Sumerian king who ruled circa 2200 BC. He wished to build a temple to honor the god Nin-Girsu and received guidance in dreams from that god about the project and when to begin it. Having problems understanding that dream, he requested and received help from the goddess Gatumdung to interpret it (so he dreamed a second dream which helped him to understand the first one.)

The library of the Assyrian king, Assurbanipal was said to have contained books about dream interpretation dating back to 2000 BC. His personal dream book was believed to be one of the chief sources for the most famous dream book of the ancient world, *Oneirocritica*, later written in Roman times.

The interpretation of dreams by priests in ancient Egypt is recorded in hieroglyphics. One surviving record tells of the pharaoh Tanuatamun (664-656 BC), an Ethiopian ruler during the decline of Egypt, having a dream of holding two snakes, one in each hand.

In ancient Greece, dreams were considered to be prophetic, giving omens of things to come. Dreams could also be used for the healing of physical ailments. Special temples called Asclepieions were dedicated to this healing work, and sick people were sent to them to incubate dreams within the bounds of these temples, invoking divine grace and in this way a cure.

The Romans were also very interested in dream interpretation. The *Oneirocritica* or *The Interpretation of Dreams,* was written in the second century AD by Artemidorus of Daldis. It was considered to be one of the first, the most famous and the most comprehensive works on the subject of dreams in the ancient world. This book included concepts such as dreams could predict the future, they could be symbolic, and that puns or plays on words could be part of the message carried by the dream.

The Bible is full of examples of dreams and dream interpretation, from Jacob dreaming of angels flying up and down a ladder to heaven, to Daniel interpreting the dreams of Nebuchadnezzar. One of the most famous dreams in the Bible is the story of Pharoah's dream of the seven fat cows and seven thin cows coming out of the Nile, and how Joseph interpreted it to foretell seven years of bounty followed by seven years of drought in the land of Egypt, thus allowing Pharoah to prepare for this and save the lives of his people.

Looking further to the East, in medieval Islamic culture, dream interpretation was widely practiced, and many books were written on the subject, including *Ta'bir al-Ru'ya* and *Muntakhab al-Kalam fi Tabir al-Ahlam* by Ibn Sirin, *On Sleep and Dreams* by Alkindus, as well as sections in the *Book of Opinions of the people of the Ideal City* by Al- Farabi, *The Cannon of Medicine* by Avicenna, and the *Muqaddimah* by Ibn Khaldun. Ibn Sirin's work is divided into 25 sections and includes such details as the etiquette of dream interpretation and the recommendation that it is better for a lay person to approach an *alim,* or Muslim scholar, for the task of interpreting a dream.

In China, one noted volume of dream interpretation is the *Lofty Principles of Dream Interpretation* written by Chen Shiyuan in the 16th century. The Chinese delved more deeply into the nature of dreaming. (One question asked in the Chinese literature of dreaming is whether one is a man dreaming he is a butterfly or a butterfly dreaming he is a man.)

At the end of the nineteenth century, one approach to dreams turned away from the spiritual and more towards the psychoanalytic. Sigmund Freud's book, *The Interpretation of Dreams,* and his work with dreams for understanding the unconscious beliefs and motivations of an individual broke new ground in the field of mental health. Freud was the first person to use the term "dream work" for using dreams to gain insight and information into a person's beliefs. Jung, Hall and other figures in the field soon developed their own approaches to dreams and their interpretation.

At the same time that Freud and his cronies were taking dreams in a psychological direction, a young man named Edgar Cayce was accessing dreams for information and healing for himself and others. Cayce, now also known as the Sleeping Prophet, had totally lost his voice, and tried hypnosis as a cure when other approaches failed. Not only did this cause his voice to return, but Edgar also found that while sleeping in a hypnotic trance, he could access his own psychic ability.

Edgar Cayce became one of the most noted American psychics of all time. For over forty years, he followed a daily practice of consciously induced psychic dreaming to:

- answer questions,
- develop alternative health remedies, and
- make predictions.

The work that Cayce did at the turn of the century is still being studied and used for people's health and well-being to this day.

More recently, in the 70s, Ann Faraday was one of those who brought dream interpretation to the mainstream by publishing do-it yourself manuals on the topic. Faraday focused mainly on the application of dreams to daily life. Other authors such as Wallace and Jean Dalby Clift continued in the 80s and the 90s to examine the nature of dreams and what they have to tell us.

As you can see, there's a lot of historical precedence for using dreaming as an effective method of psychic perception, as well as for other practical purposes. Having looked at where we've come from, let's now look at the present. Let's look at how psychic dreaming works and how we can make it work for us

Chapter 2
Pillow Talk-
Some Groundwork on
Dreams and Dream Interpretation

Let's start with talking about dreams and why we'd want to interpret them. When we sleep, most of us dream, but what are dreams anyway?

Dreams can be quite a number of things:

- Dreams can be your unconscious telling you a story about something that's happening while you're sleeping (like the story of the man who dreamt that he ate a giant marshmallow and woke up to find that his pillow was gone..)
- Dreams can be your mind having fun while you're asleep.
- Dreams can be exercise for your unconscious.
- Dreams can be stress or anxiety coming to the surface of your attention.
- Dreams can come from indigestion or physical discomfort.
- Dreams can be your mind trying to solve a problem that it can't solve when it's awake.
- Dreams can be your unconscious mind trying to get in touch with your consciousness.
- Dreams can come out of experiences, whether from ones you've remembered or forgotten.

But dreams can be also be something more.

Dreams can also be a gateway. They can be the way that your psychic ability first surfaces in your life.

I hear you thinking now.

Psychic? Who me?

13

Actually, yes, you.

I don't know if everyone is psychic. I haven't met everyone...yet; but my own experience is that every one I've encountered seems to at least have some latent degree of psychic ability or other. Most folks have had those "special" little moments:

- When you're humming a tune, turn on the radio and the same tune is playing;
- When you think of someone you haven't seen for a long time, the phone rings, and there they are;
- When you get a feeling that you should take an alternate route home, and find there was a horrendous crash on your original route;

You know, the moments like that. Those moments where you somehow know something that you just couldn't reasonably know using only the information you get through your five senses.

Psychic experiences aren't just about people foreseeing plane crashes, talking to deceased folks or predicting the "End Times".

They're also:

- the funny little things that happen every day.
- the things we know when there's no way of logically knowing them by way of the five senses.
- the "co-incidences" that we explain away with "reasons" far less likely than psychic knowledge.

And, as far as I can see, we all seem to have these experiences. These things that, when you actually think about them, can't be logically explained. These things that are easier to explain away as co-incidences, rather than look at head on. Because if we actually look at them, we may have to accept that the world is a bigger and more magical place than we previously knew- and that's scary for a lot of people.

In our culture, there are lots of folks who believe in psychic phenomena but there's not currently wide-spread acceptance of it. In other words, even though many folks privately believe that psychic abilities exist, publically it's considered unproven at best and hogwash or fraud at the worst.

At that point, if you're someone with a psychic gift, you may not know if there is anyone else like you. You may feel very alone. You may worry about what people (especially the people you care about) would think about you if they found out.

You may not know how to use or control your gift. You may not know where to go to find help to learn how to use or control your gift.

Your gift may scare you.

For that reason, many times folks will look at experiences of their sixth sense and come up with "rational explanations" to explain them. Never mind if these "rational explanations" involve amazingly unlikely factors. Never mind if those "rational explanations" don't actually make any sense.

They'll do their best to explain things all away. Because, for many of us, it's more comfortable to live in a non-magical world than it is to admit that psychic ability and magic and other such things exist...

That's understandable. We're all doing the best we can, and most of us can only handle so much at one time. It's a human thing. Unfortunately, this cuts us off from the gifts that could really help us, as well as one part of the world we live in.

Furthermore, if and when we're ready to touch the unseen, those years of being told by others and telling ourselves that "there's no such thing..." can undermine our ability to get in touch with that magical world.

We sabotage ourselves. Tell ourselves that "it's just the wind" or we're "imagining things." We tell ourselves that psychic people are special and "Who do we think we are? Isn't it conceited to think we're that special?…"

There's lots of ways to block our gifts. We block ourselves from accessing our psychic ability, and many times what is blocking us is just our sense of judgment.

Now judgment is a good thing when it's used for what it's meant for- keeping us safe from making foolish or dangerous choices.

- Not eating the leftovers that have been in the fridge a bit too long.
- Not accepting a ride from the kinda creepy stranger you've just met.
- Not giving your social security number to someone who doesn't really need it.

Those are all judgment calls, and judgment is our buddy when it's doing what it's meant to.

Sometimes, though, judgment goes overboard. In its attempt to keep us safe, it ends up blocking us from experiences that we really would benefit from, like a parent who won't let a child play with other children because he might be exposed to germs. Judgment can block us from accessing our psychic ability because:

- We've never done this before and we don't know how to do it.
- What if you see something unpleasant or frightening?
- "It isn't real. This is heading into crazy territory."
- People might think you're weird or make fun of you.
- You might fail, and failing is scary.

- And many other reasons

Its unexplored territory, and "unexplored" means "unsafe" to judgment, which may therefore want to keep you away from it. Judgment often blocks people's access to their psychic ability in a well meaning but erroneous attempt to protect them.

And this is where dreams can ride to the rescue…

Your judgment lives in your conscious mind- the part of your mind that has about 20% of the brain power. When your judgment is blocking your access to your psychic abilities, they're not gone. They're just hiding out in the unconscious mind. They're generating "hunches", and "impressions" and those funny little feelings that you can't explain but that help you immensely when you trust them. They're generating some of the "co-incidences" that we mentioned earlier in this chapter.

They're trying to get in touch with you, to give you access to your own natural psychic birth right.

And one of the earliest and clearest ways they can reach you is through dreams.

When you sleep, your conscious mind is sleeping- and that includes your judgment. The judgment that tells you "There's no such thing as psychic ability" or "You're not special enough to be psychic" or "It's not safe to be psychic."

But your unconscious mind, with all those psychic skills is still awake; and without judgment screening your calls, your psychic ability has a far better chance of getting through to you.

That's why dreams are one of the first ways our psychic ability becomes active. Because there's no one awake to tell us "No." You may go on to develop your psychic ability in other ways later on, but dreams are usually the first stop on the journey of enlightenment.

And that's why it's useful and important to learn to interpret your dreams – because they give you access to other senses you have beyond the first five. Because they give you access to information and insight that can benefit you. Because they give you access to another side of yourself that is natural and helpful to you.

That's what we're going to do next.

<u>Dream Interpretation</u>

Chapter 3
Dream Interpretation-
By the Book

As noted in the previous chapter, in the past when people had a dream that felt important to them and they wanted an interpretation of that dream, many of them would visit an oracle, priest or scholar who would interpret it for them. Later on, oracles or priests were replaced by psychiatrists, but the concept of professional guidance to interpret the messages your unconscious sent through dreams remained the same.

The concept of interpreting your own dreams is a more recent one.

These days, when I talk with people about dream interpretation, I find that the first thing they usually think of is one of those classic "dream books". You know - one of those thousands of easily available volumes you'll see lined up on the shelves in the New Age section of your local book store. They're full of convenient lists that tell you "a turkey means this" and "a blender means that" and "a sport car means the other thing" if a turkey or a blender or a sports car should happen to appear in your dreams.

Most of these books are either traditional works that go back into the dawn of time or modern reinterpretations of traditional works that go back to the dawn of time.

They're nice books. Unfortunately, though, they don't really work well for accurately interpreting your dreams ....

Say what? So what's up with that?

There's a basic problem with such guides. The problem is that most of them work on the assumption that each symbol means the same thing to every person and also that every symbol means the same thing every time. In other words, they believe that a bear always means the same thing whenever you dream about a bear, and also that no matter who is dreaming, that bear is still a symbol for the same thing.

And that's just not true.

The truth is that things that appear in your dreams are written in your own personal system of symbols. They mean what they mean to you, as opposed to what they may mean to someone else. (This is also true for meditation, visions, and other metaphysical practices.)

What do I mean by that? For instance, if I had a dream about a cat, the cat might mean "cuddly and comforting" to me, but if you dreamt about a cat, it might mean "aloof and reserved" to you. We could have two totally different meanings for the same symbol, but those meanings would both be legitimate interpretations. That's because they're based in our individual experiences of the cats in our specific dreams and of cats in general.

To give a few more examples:

- Dark could mean mystery.
- Dark could mean danger.
- Having wings could mean freedom.
- Having wings could mean disaster (as in flying too near the sun).
- A tunnel could mean transition.
- A tunnel could mean sex.
- Climbing a mountain could mean great achievements.
- Climbing a mountain could mean insurmountable obstacles.
- Work could mean purpose and meaning.
- Work could mean oppression.

As you can see from this list, any symbol has the

possibility of quite a number of different meanings, and there isn't just one "right" meaning that we can take from a book. The actual "right" meaning is the one that is right for the person who dreamt the dream. Because of this, the dreamer's own symbols and personal insight are the essential tools for the most accurate interpretation of a dream, and for getting the most useful information out of it

A classic dream book can be useful to you in the dream interpretation process, because looking at its lists of meanings of dream symbols can give you some different ideas of what a symbol in your dream might mean. It's important to remember, though, that the dream book is a list of someone else's system of symbols, and that yours may be totally different. Let that book give you some ideas- and then put it aside and listen to what your own instincts tell you about what a dream about cats or dancing or chocolate means to you. That's how you'll get your answers.

We'll be going into more detail step by step about how to do this in the chapters that are coming up. For now, please just remember that dream books can help you by giving you suggestions, but they are not an absolute authority on what your dreams actually mean.

And listen to your own feelings about what your dreams are saying.

Chapter 4
Dream Interpretation-
The Different Kinds of Dreams

Back in Chapter 2 *Pillow talk - Groundwork on Dream Interpretation*, we talked a little bit about the fact that there are all different kinds of dreams.

Not every one of your dreams is a dream generated by your psychic abilities, of course. For instance:

- Some dreams are purely physiological responses, such as when you eat pickles and ice cream too late at night and ending up having a psychedelic dream of the caterpillar in Alice in Wonderland.
- Some are just responses to your environment, like dreaming that you're in Siberia if the air \conditioning's turned down too low.
- Some of them are just your unconscious mind at play. The mind needs time to play and goof off to stay relaxed, healthy and flexible, and dreams are one way that it does this.
- Some are a pure work out for that same unconscious mind. The mind need to exercise as well as to play, and dreams will sometimes serve for this as well.
- Some are a continuation of exploring a topic, issue or question that has been preoccupying you in the waking world.
- Some are signs of stress or anxiety.
- Some are signs of health problems (ones that you already have or new ones that are on the way.)
- Some are your unconscious mind trying to remind you of things you need to know that your conscious mind has forgotten, but that are still hanging out in

your unconscious.

And there are a lot more other causes of dreams, as well...

Those are largely all dreams that come from the material world. They're physiological or purely mental in function; but dreams can also come from your innate psychic ability reaching out into the universe and bringing back information from sources that you can't access with your five senses.

So how do you know the difference between a dream that's meaningful, a dream that's physiological and a dream that's just for fun?

Well, if you have a dream, when you wake, first look for physiological or environmental causes for the dream.

- Did you dream of sleeping in a polar bear's den and wake up to find your dog had crawled in bed with you?
- Did you dream of being in the middle of a runway with planes taking off all around you, and wake to find your spouse is snoring?
- Did you dream of falling and wake up on the floor next to your bed?

If a dream is just your mind trying to make sense of your night time adventures, you want to acknowledge that and move on.

Once you've gotten past that point, your other dreams are worth examining. It's good to know that some of those dreams will just be your mind exercising or having fun, but even those dreams may have something to tell you. The most useful dreams, however, the ones for gathering helpful information tend to be the dreams that come from your psychic ability.

Let's take some time to get into the differences between playful dreams and psychic dreams in more detail now. You'll want to be able to tell the difference, so you know which ones are most helpful to work with for information and other benefits.

Psychic dreams tend to have one or more of the following aspects:

- They may feel very real to you.
- You may have problems telling if you're awake or asleep during a psychic dream.
- You may feel like you've woken up when, in fact, you're still sleeping and dreaming.
- You may wake up and have trouble telling if you're awake yet or still sleeping.
- Contrariwise, you may consciously realize that you're dreaming while you dream (but the dream will still feel very real.)
- They feel significant. (Indeed, sometimes there's an almost tangible feeling of "Pay attention - this is important" to a psychic dream.)
- They tend to stick in your memory after you wake.
- They may be recurrent. (You may have the same dream over and over.)
- They may be progressive. (You may have the same dream on multiple occasions and, each time, the story in the dream progresses a little bit further.)

Not every psychic dream has all or indeed even one of these aspects. Not every dream that has one of these characteristics is a psychic dream. That being said, these factors do often turn up in dreams sent as psychic messages and they do make good guidelines for which dreams to look more closely at.

One kind of psychic dream happens when we accidently connect with someone else's dreams, thoughts or even their waking experiences. Psychic dreams help us to connect with information that can't be reached through the five senses. There's a lot of information floating around out there, and some of it comes from lives other than our own. Sometimes we will have dreams that carry information from other peoples' lives or minds. One way to think of this is like being similar to tuning a radio to a particular channel- at most times, you're tuned into the information that's meant for you, but sometimes you may inadvertently pick up other people's information.

To figure out whether a psychic dream is actually information that belongs to someone else, pay attention to whether the dream feels like one of your own dreams. Think of a dream as being like a movie. You can usually tell the difference between a film by one director and another. You can do this with dreams as well. For most of us, our dreams have a particular feel or "flavor" to them. Even if a symbolic dream includes some pretty weird experiences, if it's your dream, it'll usually feel like it.

If you find yourself dreaming about vivid experiences that seem very real to you but do not feel like your own flavor of dreams, it's worth considering whether you're tuning into someone else's dreams. At that point, you will need to think about whether this is information that you need to have, or whether you should just shut such dreaming out. (For information on how to do this, look in chapters 13 and 14.)

Another kind of psychic dream can be a visit from beyond. Dreaming is often the way that people first get in touch with their psychic sides. In the same way, dreaming can also be the way we make contact with friends or family who have passed, spirit guides, or even contact with the divine spirit.

If all of that was not enough, psychic dreams can be divided into literal and symbolic dreams. Some psychic dreams tell us things we need to know through symbols, while some involve literally experiencing something that happened in the past, something that will happen in the future, or something that is happening far away to someone else.

Some examples of this:

- A literal psychic dream is when you dream of being dive bombed by pigeons, and are literally dive bombed by pigeons on the following day.
- A symbolic psychic dream is when you dream of being dive bombed by pigeons, and your co-workers verbally dump all over you the following day.
- A literal psychic dream is when you dream of being in a car accident, can't get the dream out of your head and thus take an alternate route to work the following day and later on find out that there was a terrible auto pileup along your usual route that day.
- A symbolic psychic dream is when you dream of being in a car accident, can't get the dream out of your head and thus double check your work on an important contract at your job, and find a mistake

that would have caused you terrible problems if you had not caught it in time.

I find that literal psychic dreams tend to happen less frequently than symbolic ones. My theory on this is that it's usually easier on a person to view a symbolic message and then interpret it, than it is to be caught in the middle of the action itself, especially if the event is traumatic or frightening. At that point, I believe that many people are more likely to consciously or unconsciously block literal dreams, than symbolic ones.

That's not always the case though. There are plenty of documented cases where folks have had literal dreams that were isolated warnings of danger to themselves or to loved ones. There are also experienced psychics who regularly have literal dreams of events to come.

Despite that, for most of us, psychic dreams seem more likely to come in the symbolic variety. Because of this and because it's usually more difficult to interpret a symbolic dream than a literal one, we'll be spending more time learning how to interpret symbolic dreams in this book.

If you have a dream of something you think might literally happen in your life, you'll want to heed that warning. It doesn't mean that you need to hide under your covers though. Just watch out, be careful and trust your instincts.

You have free will. Because of that, any dream (like any other method of predicting the future) only shows you what is most likely to happen if you keep doing things the way you've been doing them. You can always change directions and rewrite your future if you chose to take steps to do so.

Take precautions- but also take into consideration that even dreams that seem literal may actually be symbolic and here to tell you about something else altogether. Take the time to run them through the interpretation process and see what that has to tell you.

We'll be starting the process of dream interpretation in the next chapter. I'll see you there.

Chapter 5
Dream Interpretation-
the Write Stuff

Back in chapter 3 *Dream Interpretation- By the Book*, *I* talked for a bit about your classic book containing "the meanings of things in your dreams." I talked about how those books contain lists of symbols in dreams that are the symbols of the people who originally created those lists, but that may or may not have anything to do with your own personal dream symbols.

Those books may be useful in giving you ideas and options for what a symbol might mean to you, but it's very important to keep in mind that they are suggestions and nothing more than that. To truly get an accurate interpretation of your dreams, you have to determine what each symbol stands for to you.

And that means that the best person to do an accurate interpretation of your dream is you yourself, because nobody else in the cosmos will understand your own symbols better than you will. It's sometimes helpful to work with other people as a sounding board when you interpret your dream, because they can help to give you ideas and talk through your own interpretation. Keep in mind, though, that the bottom line remains that no one will be better at interpreting your dreams than you.

So how do we do that anyway?

Well, if you want to get better at dancing, you need to get out there and dance. If you want to get better at running, you need to get out there and run. And, just like running, dancing and probably pretty much everything else in this world, if you want to get good at interpreting your dreams, you need to start working with doing just that.

And as you practice interpreting your dreams, you'll

find that there are certain symbols that turn up regularly in your dreams- ones that are specific to you. Take note of these - after awhile, they'll be part of your own personal psychic shorthand, and you'll know what it means when they show up. I've included a place in this book for you to start recording your personal dream symbols in Appendix III.

To start out with practicing interpreting your own dreams, the first step is to record them. I'd recommend that you make some preparations for this so that you're ready to capture your dreams before you get to the step of interpreting them.

Set up something to write your dreams down in when you first wake up. I've included seven pages of a sample dream journal in Appendix IV of this book (That's a week's worth which is just enough to get you started out.) If you think that you'll be making this an ongoing practice, I'd recommend that you make or buy a dream journal especially for the task. You can tear the pages out of Appendix IV and punch them to clip into a ring binder, or you can buy a binder with paper or a bound journal. Copy either the prompts I've given you or other ones that you prefer into it as needed

There are some important points for your dream journal. You want something that is:

- Distinctive, so that it's easy to spot when you're half asleep but still ready to write in it.
- A convenient and comfortable size for writing in bed.
- Something that's special to you or that you'll like using, so that you'll enjoy writing in it.

- A way to clip a pen right to it is a definite bonus, as you'll need to be able to grab that pen easily when you still may be drowsy.
- While you're at it, chose a pen that feels good in your hand and is easy to write with. Put it with your journal so you're ready to go. Two nice pens are even better.

Once you've addressed these points in whatever way suits you, whatever type of journal you like the most is the right journal for you, whether it's a fancy leather bound blank book or a ring binder full of loose leaf paper.

If you don't like writing things down, or have found in the past that writing was difficult when you are still drowsy, one other alternative is something you can record your voice on. You'll want something where the controls are as simple as possible, so that you don't have to fiddle with it when you're ready to record a dream.

If you have someone who shares sleeping space with you, you might also want to think about some kind of targeted lighting, so you have enough light to write by, without waking your co-sleeper up with a flood of light.

Clear some space by your bedside so that, when you dream, the tools that you need are easily at hand and you're ready to write your dream down as soon as you wake up. Set things up so it's easy to sit up, turn on a light, grab a journal and pen and get to writing that dream down or recording it.

Many times, the more we wake up, the harder it becomes to hold onto our memories of what we've just dreamed, so you don't want to waste any time fumbling around for a pen, a recorder or your journal while the memories of your dream slide away from you.

While we're talking about dreams slipping away, I know that many people don't remember their dreams at all or at least believe that they don't remember their dreams. We'll be dealing with that later on in this book, but for now, we'll be dealing with the dreams that you do remember and doing our best to hold onto as much of them as possible.

You've got your bedroom set up. You have a journal and pens ready where they're easy to find and the light arranged so you can turn it on easily and start writing.

And then, that night, you sleep.

And that night, or the next, or the one after that, you dream.

And, when you wake, as soon as you can, sit up, turn on the light and start writing or recording. If you can manage it, try to just sit up and write, as opposed to going to the bathroom, brushing your teeth or getting some coffee first. The longer you're out of the dreaming state, the more the memories of your dream can slip away from you, especially when you first start out. That's why it's important to get started writing or recording as quickly as you can. You may find that there are things you must do first, but the sooner you can write, the more of your dream you'll have to work with.

Write down everything you can remember about the dream.

- Write down the big stuff.
- Write down the small stuff.
- Write down the weird stuff (The stuff that "doesn't seem to fit" can often be the most important part.)
- Write down things and people and objects.
- Write down things you or something else did, like running or eating or dancing the minuet.
- Write down the colors and sounds and sensations you experience.
- Write down how things made you feel. Scared? Excited? Content?
- Write down any thoughts you had during or about this dream.

Don't evaluate or judge your dream or yourself as you write. Just get it all down. The first step is to catch hold of as much of the dream as you can and preserve it on paper so that you'll have it all to sort through and find the hidden meanings in the dream later on.

Don't worry about how it looks either. If your writing is sloppy or runs all over the page because you're still half asleep, that's fine as long as you can still read what you wrote.

Be kind with yourself. Relax.

Just write. Write it all down.

And once you have all of the details of your dream, great and small, written down on that piece of paper, take a deep breath and relax. Now you can go brush your teeth or get your first cup of coffee of the day.

You've captured your dream – and in the next chapter, we're going to start working with it…

Chapter 6
Dream Interpretation-
Finding the Clues to the Hidden Story

In the last chapter, I asked to you to write down your dream in as much detail as you could. Not just the high points of the dream, but all of the specific details as well - the sensations, the feelings, the little things you notice that seem to be incidental to the dream.

In short, I want you to write down the complete story of your dream...

Sometimes dreams are literal. A dream about a lost dog or a lost love can literally be information about a lost dog or a lost love, but much of the times, dreams are symbolic. The story means that the story you first see in a dream often has another story hidden behind it. That story is what holds the actual information you need to receive.

And, when that's the case, we need to peek behind the scenes and find that hidden story.

Once you've got the original story written down, it's time to look for the real story that's hidden behind the first one. We'll start that process by identifying the key points in the original story.

The first step to looking for that hidden story? Get yourself a high-lighter, a colored marker, or any other way of emphasizing words that suits your fancy. Using color to mark your key points makes them more visible and helps the hidden story begin to appear.

Next, we're going to go through your written down dream and mark <u>any</u> element of the dream that jumps out at you.   We'll mark:

- People
- Animals
- Items
- Actions
- Descriptions
- Feelings
- Sounds
- Things that are said
- Colors
- Sensations
- Weird little things that don't seem to fit
- And so forth.

Please note that you're not just marking nouns. Verbs, adjectives or any other word that pops up in your original story may be important.

Please also note that I'm not saying "each element that seems important". Sometimes, key information is given to you by something that seems unimportant or peripheral but jumps out at you anyway. In a dream about roller skating in Central Park, the rabbit who sits quietly at a café table sipping tea may still be a key point.

And finally note that not every point in the initial dream is necessarily important. When you dream about sailing on a ship, the ship may just be the way you get from one piece of information to another

The important part is not whether an element appears center stage or not. It's more a question of, when you read over the original story of your dream, what things seem to pop out of the story at you. I tend to experience this as a feeling of alertness, the hair standing up slightly on the back of my neck, or a feeling of "yes- that's it. That's important" when I interpret a dream. You may have a totally different response - but what you'll be looking for is something in your body, mind or spirit alerting on or clicking with an element.

Let's walk through this step once right now. As an example, perhaps you have a dream like this one:

A bear is chasing you through the woods. You're running hard, frightened, exhausted. You see a house and run towards it. As you reach the front door, you see a chipmunk. You run through the door and find yourself falling through space...

41

Stop and look at the dream for a moment. What things catch your eye, or make you go "aha…" or "that's it" ?

When you looked at this dream, you might find that parts of it such as *bear, woods, running, exhausted, chipmunk, door* and *falling* were the elements that seemed to jump out at you (Your results may vary. You might find totally different things were what seemed to be key to you).

Mark each word that jumps out at you. I find that using color makes them jump out even more, which helps us to see what's really happening here. We're going to tackle each element individually, but first you have to identify them.

Got these key elements identified and marked? Good for you. Now we're ready to interpret your dream.

And that's coming in the next chapter…

Chapter 7
Dream Interpretation-
the Magic Questions, Part 1

You've dreamed…

You've written down everything that you can remember about your dream…

You've marked each and every important part or element of that dream…

And now it's time to ask the Magic Questions…

Look at each element that you marked as important in turn. Ask yourself these two simple questions:

- *What is this element to me?*

And

- *How did this element make me feel?*

That's it. That's the key.

Now I'll bet that these questions don't seem very magic to you, do they? Well, surprise! Believe it or not, even though they look ridiculously simple, these questions are the keys that unlock the secrets hidden in your dreams. I call them the Magic Questions because they seem so simple but are amazingly effective at helping you to unravel the

43

mysteries and understand what your dreams are trying to tell you.

We'll be getting into these questions in more depth in the next two chapters, but I'd encourage you to sit down with your dream and try these questions now. Trying the basic process in its simplest form has a lot to offer and can teach you quite a bit.

For each dream element, ask the magic questions and write down what you get. You may surprise yourself...

See if you can spot what your dreams are trying to tell you.

Chapter 8
Dream Interpretation-
The Magic Questions, Part 2

In the last chapter, we talked about the two magic questions of dream interpretation:

- *What does this element mean to me?*

and

- *How does this element make me feel?*

We're going look at these questions in a bit more detail now. Let's start with the first question:

What does this element mean to me?

As I've said in earlier chapters, when a dream is symbolic, it's written in your own personal system of symbols. For instance, a dream of a foggy day might mean "mystery" to one person and "depression" to another. Both would be legitimate interpretations of that dream. Which interpretation was the accurate one would depend mostly on who was having the dream, and what that symbol meant to that person.

Is that making sense?

At that point, the trick is figuring out what the symbols in your dreams mean to you. Here's how we do that. We take each symbolic dream element and free associate with it. We walk through the different things that element makes us think of. We list them off, until we find the one that feels right, or makes us think "Eureka!" or "Yes, that's it"

Let's take a walk through the process. In a previous chapter, I used the example of a dream of being chased by a bear. If this was your dream and *"**Bear**"* stood out as an important point, what does *"**Bear**"* mean to you?

Well:

- **"Bear"** is strong and powerful. Is there a situation where you feel endangered by something stronger than you?
- **"Bear"** is omnivorous, so and so can be nourished by many different situations. Do you need to learn to nurture or "nourish" yourself in more ways?
- **"Bear"** is omnivorous, and so is very flexible in his approach to the world. Do you need to be more flexible?
- **"Bear"** hibernates, so he can symbolize a need to rest.
- **"Bear"** has a traditional identity in healing work in certain cultures. Do you need more health or healing?
- **"Bears"** can come in threes (So is there a three connection with something that comes in threes? Or does that stand for three days or weeks or months?)

46

- **"Bears"** are something that you shouldn't feed. Is there a belief or situation in your life that you need to stop "feeding into" or giving your energy away to?

Keep going. Are there other things that you think of when you think about bears?

To find the meaning of the dream element, you make a list of the different associations you have with that symbol. Pay attention as you go through the possible associations. When you find the meaning, it'll jump out at you.

Signs of a symbol jumping out at you can include:

- A sudden feeling of alertness.
- The hair standing up on the back of your neck.
- An "a-ha" feeling.
- Thinking something like "That's it." Or "Yes."
- A feeling of reconnection or connection.
- Increased muscle tension.
- Increased muscle relaxation.
- Or you may have your own individual feeling, thought or sensation that lets you know when you've arrived at the right answer amongst the many answers possible.

Pay attention to what your own personal "that's it!" reaction is. Knowing what that reaction is will help you to spot it more quickly in the future and make interpretation of your dreams quicker and easier.

One other quick thing to keep in mind when using the *"What does this element mean to me?"* question is that your unconscious mind is playful and can be tricky at points. One way that it can express itself in dreams is through jokes, plays on words or puns.

As an example, **"Bear"** could be any of the meanings we came up with above; but since your unconscious may use puns or plays on words, **"Bear"** could also stand for **"Bare"** – and this could be an anxiety dream where your unconscious mind is trying to remind you that swim suit season is on the way.

Even if you hate puns, your unconscious doesn't, and they still may show up in your dreams. That's worth keeping in mind when you're looking for meanings.

You've got the first symbol identified- now go ahead and do the rest. Take each important point in this dream and work out its meaning for you. Write each one down, so you can see the pattern begin to emerge.

Please keep in mind that some symbols will be consistent for you and will always mean the same thing. You may find that, for you, a dream that includes a rose is always about romance.

Also remember, though, that while you may have some symbols always have the same meaning for you, many symbols will mean something different in each dream, dependant on the context and information that you get from the second magic question (which is coming up in the next chapter.) Keep an eye out so that you identify and write down your consistent symbols, but know that a dream crow or train or rabbit may not always stand for the same thing.

We're done with the first of the two magic questions – but we've got more to do. In the next chapter, we'll look at question number 2…

Chapter 9
Dream Interpretation-
the Magic Questions, Part 3

In the last chapter *Dream Interpretation - the Magic Questions, Part 2,* we looked at the first of the two magic questions:

- *What does this element mean to me?*

Now it's time to look at question number 2:

- *How does this element make me feel?*

Let's go back and look at each element that you marked because it jumped out at you. Stop and think about how you felt about it while you were having the dream. (It may help to close your eyes while you do this, as it can make it easier to re-experience the emotions you had at the time.) Be sure that you are looking at your feelings during the dream, as opposed to your waking feelings about this element, which may be very different.

How did this element make you feel? Think about it. Better yet, feel about it. Sometimes we need to go beyond thoughts and logic to better connect with our feelings.

Unsure what you feel? Write that down, too. When

you're working your way through this process, confusion can also be an emotional response and a clue to the hidden story that you're looking for.

Why does it matter how you feel about the things in your dreams? An element that gives you a positive feeling means something very different from the same element paired with a negative feeling. An element that creates a strong feeling in you can be quite different from one that generates a vague emotion.

As one example, let's take a look at the sample dream from chapter 7 that we've been working with. If a bear is chasing me in a dream and I feel scared of the bear chasing me, it's may be standing for something that I don't want to look at in my waking life. On the other hand, if I'm dreaming that I'm giggling while being chased by the identical bear, then one interpretation is that something big is coming my way that is not as intimidating or scary as it looks...

When you look at that, do you see how your feelings about the different symbols can change the actual meaning of the dream? ...

To review, the basic process up to this point is:

- You write down your dream.
- You identify each important part or key element.
- You look at those important elements.
- You look at what this element means to you.
- You look at how it makes you feel.
- You write down the meanings and feelings you harvest from looking at the original story of your dream.

And, having done these steps, you've now got the information that you need to interpret your dream.

And that's what we're doing in the next chapter- revealing the story hidden behind the story…

Chapter 10
Dream Interpretation –
the Story Behind the Story

We've dreamed…

We've written down that dream…

We've marked each important aspect that jumped out at us…

We've asked the two magic questions-

- *What is this element to me?*

And

- *How does this element make me feel?*

We've written down our answers to those questions…

And now we're ready to really look at those answers and to see the story that emerges from them. We're ready to interpret the dream.

Look at your notes on what all of the different dream elements meant to you and how they made you feel. See how they fit together and what kind of patterns they form.

If these hidden meanings were telling you a story, what would it be?

As you look at the hidden meanings and at the patterns they make, you'll gradually see a new story emerging. Your story- the story that's hidden behind the story of the original dream.

This hidden story is what your symbolic dream is trying to tell you.

To illustrate this process in more detail, let's run through it with our sample dream from chapter 6 *Dream Interpretation- Finding the Clues to the Hidden Story.*

A bear is chasing you through the woods. You're running hard, frightened, exhausted. You see a house and run towards it. As you reach the front door, you see a chipmunk. You run through the door and find yourself falling through space...

In this dream, let's say that the key elements are **bear, running, exhausted, chipmunk, door,** and **falling.** (Your mileage may vary- your key elements may be totally different...)

Now, if this were my dream/being expressed in my symbolic dream language, it would mean this.

- *The bear* (which stands, in this case, for hibernation or a need to sleep) is chasing me.
- I'm *running* (meaning I'm avoiding the fact that I need more rest.)
- I'm *exhausted* (meaning that I'm at the end of my energy or personal resources.)
- I reach a *door* (which stands for a significant point in my life or entering a new phase of my life. This is one of my more consistent personal symbols.)
- I see a *chipmunk.* (Another personal symbol. Chipmunks tend to be symbols of luck for me, so the chipmunk stands for potential good fortune or benefits if I pay attention.)
- I'm *falling* (in this case, this stands for getting sick because I'm short of sleep and worn out.)

So, if this were my dream, the hidden story would be that I'm in desperate need of additional rest or sleep, and that, if I do not get more sleep, I will get sick. It also adds that I still have time to choose a more fortunate option (a chipmunk) and, by choosing to take action, avoid getting sick.

So I think I'll go take a nap now…

See how that works?

Now try it with a dream of your own.

You may be surprised at what stories emerge when you peek behind the veil.

One way of making this process simpler is to get yourself a dream buddy or buddies- one or more people who would also like to learn to interpret their own dreams. While you can learn to interpret your own dreams, and you are ultimately the person who is best able to accurately interpret your own dreams, working with others has many benefits, especially when you're starting out.

- Talking through your original dream with your dream buddies can help you remember more details. Telling the story to others makes it clearer in your own head.
- Telling the story to your dream buddies can also help you to zero in on what the key elements are in the original dream.
- Dream buddies can help you make a list of different possible meanings for key elements, until you find the one that makes you think "Yes! That's it!"
- Dream buddies can help you keep track of key elements that you might otherwise forget about.
- Making a commitment to work with others can help you be more consistent in continuing to work with your dreams.
- And it can be a lot of fun (and fun is good for you, in addition to feeling good.)

Some folks prefer to work on things alone, while others prefer to work with other people. If you like company on your journey to insight, you may want to see if you have friends who might also like to interpret their own dreams and would like to be your dream buddies.

Right now, this whole process for dream interpretation may seem somewhat daunting to you. It may seem like a long and complicated process with a lot of steps to it. It may seem like a lot of work to do just to interpret a dream.

Have faith. It only seems this complex when you're starting out. As you get used to it, the whole process gets simpler.

To begin with, I'm having you write things down and mark them while you're starting because it makes the steps more concrete and the aspects, their meanings and the patterns they form when you put them together more visible and easier to see. Writing things down keeps you from missing details and makes the whole process clearer.

With practice, though, you'll be able to fly through the same process in your head (which does save a lot of both time _and_ trees…)

You may still want to write your dreams down though, even after you have gotten good at the process.

Why?

- Some folks like a record of what they dreamed and their interpretations
- Some people like to keep a record of what happened that seems to link back to their dreams.
- Some dreams predict long-term things and a record can be very handy in such cases because it can help you to see connections you might otherwise miss.

- A record of your dreams and interpretations can give you confidence in the process and in your own inner wisdom.
- A record of your dreams and interpretations can help you to learn the process faster, and give you more insight into how it can help you.
- Most simply, a dream record can help you to see that this process works and that your dreams are helpful to you.

Short term, a dream journal is a useful and helpful tool. Long term, whether you use a dream journal or not depends a lot on what you want to do with your dreams- and just like interpreting them, you're the best judge of what will work for you.

You've got the process- so the next step is to try it out on your own dreams.

But what if you can't remember them?

Interestingly enough, there's a way to deal with that.

And we'll be looking at it in the next chapter....

Dream Work

Chapter 11
Dream Work-
But I Don't Remember My Dreams...

We've just spent a lot of time looking at symbolic dreams- what they are, how they work and how to receive the information that they're bringing to us.

But what if you don't dream? Or what if you dream but don't remember your dreams?

Don't worry. We're dealing with that next.

Truth be told, most people do dream. Indeed dreaming seems to be an essential part of a healthy sleep cycle. Sleep studies that monitor the different kinds of electrical activity in the brain show that dreaming is going on in the majority of us, even if we don't remember it.

Full dreaming tends to occur during the R.E.M. (Rapid Eye Movement) part of sleep. With very few exceptions, most people experience R.E.M. at least once per sleep cycle (whether that is a full 8 hours or even during many naps throughout the day), so electrical brain monitoring during sleep indicates that most of us are really dreaming on a regular basis.

The problem for most of us doesn't seem to be whether we dream or not. The problem seems more about remembering the dreams that we do have.

Many people don't remember their dreams. Some not only don't remember the actual dreams themselves, but also sleep so deeply that they don't even remember that they've dreamed at all.

That seems like a kind of impasse there. If you can't remember your dreams, or even that you have dreamed, you can't interpret them, right?

There's a way of working around that, though...

First, when you're planning on interpreting your dreams, be sure you've got your dream journal or other appropriate writing materials (pad and pencil/crayon and sketch pad/ birch bark and quill dipped in crushed berries /whatever floats your boat) right next to the bed, so you're ready to record.

As we've noted before, when passing from dreaming to waking state, you come through several different levels of brain waves. If, on top of that, you visit the bathroom, go get a drink, then have to hunt around for something to write on, you might as well kiss that dream goodbye now and save yourself the trouble.

Ready to record your dreams? Then when you get into bed and are drifting off to sleep, tell yourself "Tonight, I will dream and I will remember my dream..."

(You don't have to use these exact words, of course. Something similar to it that uses words that work for you will do just fine. Just make sure that you hit the two major points - dreaming and remembering.)

Repeat this statement over and over again as you fall asleep, so it can gently sink into your mind and drop down into your unconsciousness.

If you sleep alone, you can do this out loud if you like. If you share sleeping quarters, do this silently in your mind. (It'll work just as well).

The primary reason to use the silent method is because you don't want to weird out your sleep buddy - plus it's far harder to dream if said buddy keeps thumping you with a pillow and saying **"Will you hush up?!?!"**

How does this work? Well, it's all about brain waves and the programming in your unconscious mind. As you pass from full waking alertness (Beta waves) down through Alpha, Theta and Delta waves, your mind becomes more receptive to suggestions that you give to yourself. (For a quick reference to this, check *Appendix I Brain Waves* later on in this book.) Your mind, deep down, knows exactly how to remember your dreams. You're just, in effect, retraining your body to remember.

For the record, this is an extremely simple form of self-hypnosis. For anyone reading this who may be worried or weirded out by the concept of hypnosis, let me give you a couple of quick bits of information that may help to put your mind at ease.

- One- You cannot be hypnotized to do something against your own will. (The people who flap like chickens at hypnosis shows are usually people who have gone there with the expectation of "losing control" and doing something "over the top" and this goes along with doing something silly, just for fun.
- Two - If someone were to try to hypnotize you to do something against your free will, you'd snap right out of the hypnotic trance (and probably say something less than courteous to them in the process.)
  I know this from my own personal experience. At one point, I was trying out hypnosis tapes as part of a class. Now, when I'm hypnotized, I usually go deep into hypnotic trance, so deep that I don't always remember everything that's said to me. In this case, however, when the voice on one tape that

was guiding the session started saying things that went against my own personal values, I instantly snapped from almost asleep to wide awake, alert and cranky.

- Three - Even if it were possible to control someone through hypnosis, in this case, since you're the one in charge, you're the one that chooses what to tell your unconscious mind to believe. So you're the one driving the car of your mind- which is a good thing.

Overall, self hypnosis is a safe way to clear out negative beliefs (like "I can't remember my dreams"), replace them with helpful beliefs (like "I can remember my dreams"), and activate the part of your unconscious mind that is more than willing to put you in touch with your inner wisdom through your own dreaming.

This programming for remembering your dreams may work pretty quickly, or it may take more time to work. That's based on parameters such as how deep you sleep, how receptive you are to your own suggestions, how much your sleep buddy hits you with that pillow, and so forth. The bottom line is that, if you keep doing it, you will begin to remember your dreams.

And, lucky you! You just happen to know how to interpret them.

But what if you run up against a dream that is confusing and mysterious? What if you dream a dream that you can't find the meaning of?

We'll find the answers to that in the next chapter…

Chapter 12
Dream Work-
"Answers Unclear"....

In the last chapter, we looked at the concerns of folks who don't remember their dreams. We also examined the concerns of folks who don't know if they even dream at all.

You might even be one of those people...

We talked about dreams happening as part of the R.E.M. (rapid eye movement) period of sleep, and the fact that, since most of us experience R.E.M., most of us <u>are</u> dreaming, whether we remember it or whether we go so deep into the realms of sleep that we do not.

I went into a simple method of self hypnosis to reprogram yourself to remember your dreams by connecting with your unconscious mind as you drop off to sleep.

Is everyone up to speed?

Good!

Now let's build on that.

_____

In the first part of this book, we've talked a lot about how dreams are often messages from your intuition or your unconscious mind. For most of us, until we consciously make a choice to contact our inner wisdom and actively work with it, our psychic ability stays hidden in our unconscious.

Dreams are basically the way that your psychic self first pokes its head up and says "Hello. I'm here. Are you ready to be friends with me yet?"

We've talked about the different kinds of dreams.

We've talked a lot about symbolic dreams and the easiest way to successfully interpret your own individual dream symbols.

Well enough.

But what if you tend to get dreams full of obscure symbols that you just can't find a meaning for?

- What if sugar plum moose in lavender tutus cha cha through the drive thru lane of your dreams?
- What if you dream of doing the back stroke for miles and miles through a sea of peppermint schnapps?
- What if, while you sleep, you happen to encounter Albert Einstein, who takes one look at you, shouts "Aha!" and then runs off into the surrounding darkness?
- What then?

A personal disclaimer here- these dreams are not necessarily ones that I have ever had.

(Although it's just possible that I might have. You never know...)

And I've certainly never heard of anyone else who has had these specific dreams.

I'm just having fun with examples. You gotta take your fun where you can find it.

What if you have those wild and wacky dreams and you just can't seem to pin down what they're trying to tell you?

Well, there's a simple solution to confusing dreams and obscure dream symbols.

Remember how, in the last chapter, we programmed ourselves to remember our dreams? How we told ourselves as we dropped off to sleep" Tonight I will dream and I will remember my dreams?..."

Well, we can add things on to that.

Are you vexed by a chronic pattern of dreaming dreams full of obscure symbols? Is it bugging you that your psychic ability is trying to tell you something and you just can't figure out what it is?

Then do this.

As you drop off to sleep, tell yourself (silently or out loud, dependant on your situation…)

- "Tonight, I will dream."
- "I will remember my dreams."
- "And my dreams will come to me in symbols that I easily and clearly understand.…"

(Once again, please remember that you don't have to use these exact words. Just choose something that suits you and hits those three basic ideas of dreaming, remembering and symbols that are understandable and clear to you.)

Simple, no?

But, very effective.

This may work for you immediately. It may take some time. (Everybody's different- thank goodness!) But it will work.…

And then you can start more easily getting benefits out of what your dreams have to tell you.

There's more dream work coming up.

Chapter 13
Dream Work-
Night Time Visits

And now for something a little bit different.

Back in *Chapter 4- Dream Interpretation- the Different Kinds of Dreams,* I touched briefly on the concept that sometimes dreams are visits from folks from beyond the veil. I'd like to go into that a little bit more now.

As we've previously discussed, many of us have our first psychic experiences through dreams. That's because, while we're sleeping, the judgment in the conscious mind is asleep. It's not able to tell us things like "there's no such thing as psychic ability..." or "you're making this all up" or "who are you to think you're so special?..." Your unconscious mind, on the other hand, continues wide awake even when you sleep, and able to use the psychic powers that hang out there until you learn to use them consciously.

Just as dreams are the way that many of us first make contact with our psychic sides, so also are they the ways that many of us first have contact with non- physical beings. Whether guides or totems or the spirits of the people we love who have passed, dreams offer a connection with those on the other side of the veil, without fighting with the judgment that may tell us "you can't do that!..."

Let's take a quick look at some of the folks that we may meet in our dreams.

Some folks have spirit guides- non-corporeal helpers who come to them in dreams or visions. A guide may do things like bring you information, help you learn how to do things in the world of dreams, or keep you safe while you're dreaming. Many spirit guides are first seen in dreams, but, if you work with them, you may be able to contact them while awake when you have more experience.

Some people work with totems in dreams and visions. A totem is usually an animal spirit that works in a shamanic framework with you. It embodies certain characteristics such as strength, wisdom, or patience, and can do many of the things that a spirit guide can.

Some people, while dreaming, encounter people that they love who have died. An encounter with a loved one may be brief (maybe once) to tell you that they're ok, but many people report friends or family members who visit them regularly in dreams, offering support, insight or comfort.

And, just as a psychic dream can be literal or symbolic, likewise, a person in a dream can be literal or symbolic. Sometimes our loved ones drop by to say hi while we're dreaming. Sometimes, a dream visit is a message being framed in terms of advice we can trust, just as we trusted that person.

So, how do you tell if a visitor in a dream is a literal

spirit visit, a symbol of the relationship you had, or just your unconscious getting some exercise?

I'd say that the best way to do this is to listen to what your intuition and your body has to tell you. Do you remember back in *Chapter 8- Dream Interpretation- the Magic Questions part 2,* where I talked about the signs of a symptom jumping out at you?

As a quick refresher:

- A sudden feeling of alertness.
- The hair standing up on the back of your neck.
- An "a-ha" feeling.
- Thinking something like "That's it." Or "Yes."
- A feeling of reconnection or connection.
- Increased muscle tension.
- Increased muscle relaxation.
- Or you may have your own individual feeling, thought or sensation that lets you know when you've arrived at the right answer amongst the many answers possible.

When you listen to your instincts and your body, you get a feel for what your own personal "that's it!" signs are, and those can serve you in situations like this as well.

If you have a dream with visitor in it, think about that dream with an open mind. Do you feel like this was an actual visit? A symbolic dream? Or just some random dream play?

Watch for your own reactions and trust what they have to tell you. That's part of the process of opening to your own intuition.

If you need a little more confirmation and someone visits you regularly in dreams, it's also ok to ask for confirmation of whether it's an actual visit or not. Ask for some information that you don't know but can confirm.
(date of birth or marriage, what school she attended, or something like that.) There are some things that a spirit may not be permitted to share, but it's still ok to ask for some confirmation.

A dream visit from someone from the spirit world may feel startling at first, but that's only because you aren't used to it. Once you have experience, such a visit can be both comfortable and useful to you. It's worthy of note, on the other hand, that sometimes you may feel uncomfortable for a reason.

Just like in the physical world, not everyone in the spirit world is kind or has your best interests at heart. While the dream world is not like some Hollywood horror film, full of nasties looking to do bad things, there are some spirits who are mischievious, dishonest or who will do you a bad turn if they get the chance.

If you have a dream with a visitor, and that visitor makes you feel uneasy, it's good to trust your instincts, just as you would in the waking world. Only listen to visitors that your instincts feel good about. If a visitor makes you uneasy, there are ways to "end the conversation"

- Tell them firmly that they are no longer welcome.

(This sounds silly, but it's surprising how often it works, especially if you're firm.)

- Prayer is often effective at closing the door to visitors crashing your dreams.
- Sprinkling a circle of salt around the room or your bed can make a barrier to unwanted energy.
- Or, you can use the dream programming we've already used in other ways to program to be visited only by those who have our best interests at heart. More on this in the next chapter.

The point is that you're not required to dream host anyone who stops by. Just the ones that you'd like to talk to.

So what's the point of having dream visitors?

Sometimes they're here just to touch base after they've passed on. Sometimes they're here to work with us. Sometimes they're here so we can enjoy the relationship. There are as many reasons for a dream relationship as there are for a waking one, and it's up to the both of you to work out what your relationship is about.

It's good to remember that love doesn't end when we die. Sometimes that's why we have visitors in our dreams.

Whether it's a quick drop-by or an ongoing working relationship while you sleep, the presence of visitors in your dreams can be helpful and rewarding. Be sure to choose who you let spend time with you in your dreams, just like you would choose in the waking world; and then enjoy your dream world company.

Chapter 14
Dream Work –
Troubled Sleep

We've covered a lot of ground on dreams and dream work so far. We've talked about psychic dreams, how to interpret your dreams, techniques for working with your dreams and so forth. There's still a lot more to look at about working with your dreams, but I'm going to diverge from that for a chapter or two.

We know that psychic ability first tends to surface for most of us in our dreams, because, when we're asleep, our judgment is also asleep and therefore is not around to tell us that being psychic isn't possible.

This concept can help us to access out psychic side and is an idea that can be very helpful to us in an assortment of ways.

But, what about those times when psychic dreaming isn't always helpful?

- When it's disruptive?
- When it's scary?
- When it's just plain inconvenient?
- When it tells you things that you really would rather not know? (As in, time out- over sharing…)

Do psychic dreams have a downside? (And how can we best deal with that?)

I got an email from a person who'd been following some posts that I'd made about how to work with psychic dreams. He was dealing with a different side of psychic dreaming. He was often getting information that was unnecessary to him, unwanted, and overly personal. Things like who's sleeping with whom, what were other peoples' family traumas or catastrophes that happened in the distant past.

Not fun, this.

So what do you do when you're dealing with "none of my business" or "I don't want to know" problems in psychic dreaming?

- When you dream about things that you can't do anything about (such as catastrophes that are happening while you dream and are on the other side of the globe)?
- When you dream about things that are overly personal or not really your business (such as people's personal problems, sex lives or medical issues)?
- When you have visitors in your dreams that you just don't want there?
- When you dream about things that are traumatic to you and leave you physically, emotionally and spiritually drained (such as dreaming about people dying in car accidents or in fires?)
- When you can't get a good night's sleep because of all of the psychic traffic coming through your dreams and are exhausted for the day to come?
- When you have psychic dreams that exhaust you on night after night after night; and your health begins to suffer from long term lack of sleep?

What do you do then?

Well, some people try consciously or unconsciously to shut down their psychic gift.

Now, there are a number of good reasons to shut down a psychic gift temporarily. Sleep deprivation is one of the better ones. Sleep deprivation can depress your immune system and make you vulnerable to illness, cut your effectiveness in the waking world, and make you less alert and therefore more vulnerable to accidents and mistakes. It also feels rotten, and makes you cranky and no fun to be with. Because of that, it can hurt your relationships with the folks around you.

Unfortunately, shutting down the psychic ability that's breaking through via dreams is only workable as a temporary solution.

For most folks, when they try to shut down their psychic ability, they mainly either try to ignore it, stuff it down so deep in the unconscious through denial that they can't hear it well, or medicate themselves enough (through drinking or through sleeping pills, for instance) that they can no longer hear their own inner wisdom.

But their psychic self is still there. Still functioning. And it has a tendency to re-surface or break past those blocks either:

- During periods of highest stress and challenge (such as when you're caught in some kind of dangerous crisis, like an earthquake.)
  At such a time, you may start once more receiving messages through dreams or other methods
  to help you to adapt, make better decisions
  and survive.
  Or else:
- When you're stressed and exhausted and your own personal control is at its lowest levels (such as when you've been seriously ill or depressed for a significant amount of time.)
  At such a time, your personal resources and ability

to control yourself are at low ebb, and the energy you have been using to hide your psychic abilities from your waking self may no longer be available to you.

Your psychic ability is just trying to help you to survive and to cope better with extreme situations. Unfortunately, if you've never worked with it in situations when you have the time and energy to get to know how it works, during a crisis or low ebb situation is a hard time to get up to speed.

That being said, if the dreams are coming too quickly or taking more out of you than you have to give, shutting them down can be workable as a short term coping strategy.

Just until you've learned how to work with your dreaming. It's far better to learn how to manage and gain control over your gift, so it can serve you as it was meant to.

While we're talking about this, did you know that you're not required to take in every single dream that floats by?

It's true.

Some dreams contain information that is distinctly meant for you specifically, but many dreams are just generated by your exposure to energy that's floating around the cosmos. You're not required to experience every plane crash, or crime, or other person's mental problem solving in the dream world, or lost hiker that's floating around in the aether.

You can choose what kinds of dreams you're willing to accept- and what kinds you're not.

With that in mind, did you know that you:

- Can set parameters on incidents of psychic input? (For example: I only have psychic dreams only when I consciously declare that I am willing   to receive them.)
- Can, in effect, set "office hours" which are the only time you're willing to receive psychic dreams? (For example: no non-emergency visions while I am commuting, or I only receive psychic dreams on the weekend.)
- Can set limitations on the kind of info you're willing to receive? (For example: not to share other people's romantic encounters.)
- Can set limitations on what can happen where? (For example: no dreams of deceased folks in messy condition in my bedroom.)
- Can say that certain types of dreams or dream visitors are not permitted. Period.

And other specific parameters such as that.

It's your psyche. You get to choose who and what gets to visit you.

As another example, I don't tend to have a lot of dreams about world disasters. While those are very important events, there's not very much I can do about most of them, so I've chosen not to admit the pain and sorrow of those experiences that I cannot change into my dreams. I may still have dreams regarding local or personal events, where it might have some benefit to myself or others, but I don't dream dreams that will cause me pain with no good reason.

Want to set parameters and limits on your psychic dreaming so it can be helpful without exhausting you? There's a number of ways to do this sort of thing. The simplest way is one that you already know about...

When you go to sleep, you can give yourself

directions defining what kind of psychic dreaming you will accept and what kinds you will not. Such as:

- "I only have psychic dreams when I consciously ask to…"
Or
- "I only dream of information that applies directly to me"
Or
- "My psychic dreams come in ways that support my health and happiness."
Or
- "I only have psychic dreams about something that I can do something about."
Or
- "The morning after a psychic dream, I am always healthy and well-rested."

Or whatever specific parameters for dreaming will create a situation that is useful and helpful to you, as opposed to letting psychic input overwhelm you with too much information, leaving you exhausted.

You don't have to only choose one parameter either. You can choose as many conditions as seem necessary and appropriate for you to be able to live with and use your psychic gift in your life.

When you're doing this programming for the kinds of dreaming that you will accept, it is important to always make these statements positive. (For example, "After a psychic dream, I am always healthy and well-rested." as opposed to "After a psychic dream, I am not tired.")

For some reason, the unconscious mind does not consistently hear negative words such as "no", "not", "never" and the like. Because of this, it tends to edit out these words and "I am *not* tired." becomes "I am tired."

And that interferes with what you are trying to accomplish.

So keep your statements positive.

At the end, the important thing to remember is that you can access your psychic abilities through your dreams...

And you that you always have the ability to choose what kind of dreams you want to allow into your life.

- How often you're willing to dream.
- When you're willing to dream.
- What kind of dreams you're willing to have.
- Whether you are willing to receive personal information through dream or not.
- Under what circumstances you wish to dream.
- Whether dreaming informs you or exhausts you.
- Whether to dream so much that it has an effect on your health or not.

The choice is always yours. Now there's a useful thought.

Chapter 15
Dream Work -
And More Troubled Sleep

As we said in the last chapter, often psychic dreams are helpful because they can give us the information we need to make more informed decisions; but sometimes, they can actually interfere with our waking lives in a less than helpful way.

There are some times we will want to set long term or permanent parameters, such as no dreams of nuclear explosions, or the stock market, or dream time visits from boring conversationalists who are deceased but who ramble on and on and on anyway.

And sometimes you may need to make temporary changes in your rules for psychic dreaming, based on your personal situation, ones that you can change again later as your life itself changes.

What might make that a good idea?

There are times in life when you need all of your energy, your alertness and your focus to be on the situation in front of you in the physical world. At such times, some dreams may bring you information that is helpful for your current situation, but others may pile too many other things on your plate that you're not able to deal with at the present time; or may demand so much energy to experience the dream that you may not have enough left to deal with the following day.

At that point, you may choose to limit your psychic dreams to what is immediately pertinent to you, or even to stop having psychic dreams for a couple of days, while you rest up and gather your strength. Some examples of times when you might chose to limit your psychic dreaming or even not have a psychic dream at all that particular night include:

- The night before an important meeting or big test (when you want to be well rested and focused on the task at hand.)
- When you're sick. (Illness can throw bizarre and inaccurate twists into dreams, and a vivid and active psychic dream can wear you out and prevent you from getting the rest that you need to heal.)
- During shared intimate experiences such as sex, death or childbirth. (There's such a thing as too much closeness...)
- When there's nothing that you can do. (If there is a disaster on the other side of the planet, sending funds may be helpful and volunteering for a relief group may be helpful, but suffering through dreams that recreate the experience is probably not.)
- When you need to be dreaming your own dreams, as opposed to someone else's. (Sometimes psychic dreams happen when our minds tune in to the same wave length as someone else's dreams or waking experiences.)

There may be times when it's a good idea to use the suggestion technique that we've been using for dream programming to say that tonight's not really a good night for a psychic dream.

To keep your gift alive, you do need to continue to use it, but you don't necessarily need to use it all of the time. Given that fact, it's often good to think about things at bedtime and consciously chose whether to open yourself to psychic dreams or not.

This not only develops balance, so you get the rest that you need, but also starts developing your control over your more general psychic abilities- control that you'll be glad to have later along. (Remember when I said that dreams are often the way that your psychic ability comes out to play first?...)

It's also a good idea to incorporate a suggestion that, if this is a "non-dream" night, and there is urgent information that you need immediately for your own safety, health and well-being; or that of someone you care for, that the information will come through immediately and clearly ("...This Night Is Pre-Empted For A Special Report...")

So strike the balance between psychic information and rest, and have a wonderful night and a wonderful day besides...

Chapter 16
Dream Work-
The Five More Minutes Technique

So far we've been using techniques for programming your dreams mainly to work on the act of dreaming itself - to remember your dreams, to make them easier to interpret, to control the kinds of dreams you receive both short term and long term.

Now we're going to expand the use of that technique- to open it up for other, more general useful applications.

Do you (like me) love to hit the snooze bar on the alarm clock for "Five more minutes..." of sleep?

Well, now you can use that delicious period of additional snoozing to gain more direct access to your own personal psychic ability.

Got a question, problem or issue that you're chewing over but just can't seem to resolve? Want to tap into your natural intuition for more insight?

Let's try the "Five minutes more..." dream work technique...

For this technique, you need:

- An alarm clock with a snooze bar.
- The ability to hit that snooze bar and go back to sleep again.
- A morning when you can sleep as late as you like.
- Sufficient fatigue to do so.
- Understanding housemates who will not insist that you "get up right now".

(Sounds like fun already, right?)

The night before you want to do this technique, you need to prepare for it. Before going to sleep, set the alarm to wake you at a time when you think you will be rested, but still able to drop easily back into slumber. (An approximate "guess-timate" of this time is absolutely fine for this.)

The following morning, when the alarm sounds, hit the snooze bar, and then, go back to bed.

Allow yourself to drop off to sleep again, thinking about the question that you're trying to sort out.

And watch now for the little dreams that are likely to pop up in those five (or six or eight…) minutes.

If you dream during this period, you'll often find that you have vivid dreams that will give you pertinent and useful information on your issue, once you have interpreted them (and we all know how to do that here, don't we?..)

So, just how does this work?

- By having just come out of sleep and then turning around and diving right back in, you're still in a brain wave state of alpha/theta or even a touch of delta. This is where your intuition naturally hangs out.
- Because it's likely that you've just come out of the dream state, you're still already half-way there. Therefore, it's easier and quicker for you to get back in again.
- By thinking about your question as you drop back to sleep, you're programming your unconscious mind to gain access to information on your question.
- By only allowing yourself the length of a snooze cycle (or two, if you hit "snooze" one more time), you allow yourself to go just deep enough to dream, but don't go deep enough that you can't remember your dreams.

To a certain extent, this technique lets you combine the control of the conscious state with the intuition of your unconscious mind.

If you do this on a regular basis, you'll condition your unconscious to find answers to your questions for you on request whenever you ask for them. You'll find yourself able to focus-dream the answers you need more easily and consistently.

You may also find that you begin to get more voluntary access to your psychic abilities when you are awake as well.

And who couldn't use that?

Give it a try and see what happens.

And then join me in the next chapter for ideas on what to do when the physical world gets in the way of your dreaming…

Chapter 17
Dream Work-
Getting Back In

So you've been doing dream work. You've been doing it on an ongoing basis so you can learn how to be better at tapping into your own inner wisdom; and it's going well.

And then something goes wrong.

You're having one of those important dreams...

You know, the one that holds the missing piece of information that you need. The one that's been hiding out in your subconscious or in the Cosm that lies beyond...

You're just about to see the answer...

You can feel it there, just beyond the edge of your sight...

You're feeling excited as the answer begins to emerge from the depths of your inner knowing...

....

....

And then the alarm rings. The dog jumps on the bed. You get a cramp in your calf.

And the dream slips out of your reach.

It's gone. You almost saw it, but not quite. You can tell it was just what you needed but now you can't even remember it, try as you will.

******

******

Stay calm.

Don't panic.

We can fix this.

Get up now, turn off the alarm, visit the facilities and do whatever else needs immediately doing.

Keep your visual focus soft. If you normally wear glasses, see if you can do without them for the moment.

Try not to talk or think too much, or interact with other people or your environment any more than you absolutely have to. The more that you focus on things in the physical world, the more you pull yourself out of dreaming. The more you can stay in that half-awake state, the easier it'll be to return to the dream.

And, as soon as you possibly can, return to bed. Many times lying down in the same position that you woke up in can be helpful, if you remember what that position was.

And now we're going to get back in, and find your dream again...

Here's how we do it:

- Close your eyes.
- Take a deep breath.
- Relax your muscles.
- Cast your mind back to the last bit of the dream that you can remember.
- And set your intent to continue the dream from where you left off...

That's it. Another pretty simple technique. Another pretty simple technique that works, surprisingly enough.

If you haven't heard the phrase before, "setting your intent" is just a fancy-schmancy new age kind of term for setting a goal or objective. (This is a principle that most metaphysical activities are based on.)

If the concept of goals or objectives is a bit too high pressure for you, all that we're really doing here is focusing on what we want to do, because focusing helps us to go there and get back into our dreams again.

Most of all, please don't panic. Relax. Don't force it - let it happen. The adrenalin rush that goes with trying too hard is the exact opposite of the ideal conditions for returning to the dream state.

So let go and let it flow...

Many times, this is all that you need to get back in and reclaim or finish your dream. Sometimes it isn't. If you don't get back in within fifteen to twenty minutes or so, get up and do something else for a while. Then try again later. This lets your mind sneak up on the dream if it's playing coy.

And know that you'll get there eventually.

This is another technique that you can use during those lazy, cozy snooze alarm sessions. You can use it when the physical universe breaks you out of a dream, but you can also use it to build your ability to remember the act of dreaming, remember your dreams and actively use your dreams to access your inner wisdom, answer your questions and give you insight.

All in all, it's generally handy.

And, once you've got this technique under your belt, the next chapter takes you into the realms of using your dreams to boost your creativity....

Chapter 18
Dream Work-
Programming Your Dreams for Creativity

We've talked about dream interpretation, and programming your dreams to let you access your own natural psychic ability at will. We've talked about dreaming for insight and answering questions.

Now we're going to take this in a slightly different direction. Let's take a look at using your dreams to help you to access your own creativity. This is a technique that will work for all creative types, from artists, to actors, to people who are trying to find a better way to problem solve and think outside of the box, but, since I'm functioning as a writer at the moment, I'm going to talk about this primarily from that direction.

Having problems getting ideas for projects? Written yourself into a corner? Just can't pick the right colors to get the effect you're looking for? Problems expressing your character's inner conflicts so your audience connects with her? Writer's block? Need insight into a character, plot twist, or where your story is going next? Know the same solutions that haven't worked before won't solve a problem, but can't come up with a new and effective approach? These are all challenges that dream programming can help you with.

How can dreams help us to better access our creativity? The unconscious holds a lot of the power of the brain, including a lot of the more instinctive or intuitive types of creativity. It's all in there.

Many of the blocks we have in creative processes such as writing are caused by judgment (which is found primarily in the conscious part of the brain). If we bypass the conscious mind and go straight to the unconscious, we can avoid these blocks and tap more directly into our own natural creativity.

And one of the easiest ways to do this is through dreams.

What are the steps to dream programming?
First, know what you want.

- Do you have a specific topic or question? Be clear on what you're looking for.
- Are you just "stuck"? Intend to dream the information you need to move forwards in your creative project.
- Are you doing work that's boring or just "blah"? Intend to find the most interesting or exciting way to approach or present your subject.

Make your objective or intention for your dream as specific as you need, and no more so. If what you want is how to get out of the corner you've written yourself into, ask for that, and not how your hero tricks the villain.

Sometimes your creativity will come up with something unexpected. Leave it some wiggle room to receive that surprise answer, rather than block it by too narrow parameters.

Once your intention is clear, and you're drifting off to sleep in bed, simply tell yourself repeatedly:

- "Tonight, I will dream a dream that will help me to (insert intention here)."

- "When I wake, I will remember my dreams."
- "I will dream in symbols that I will easily and clearly understand…."

As previously noted, if you sleep alone, you can do this out loud. If you share sleeping quarters, do this in your head. (It'll work just as well.)

Also as we've said before, you don't need to use these exact words. You can change them if you want to. The important part is to hit the key points in your intentions. The first suggestion programs you to dream with purpose. The second one to remember your dreams. The third suggestion sets an intention that you clearly understand the information that your dreams bring you.

When you wake, sometimes you may instantly know what your dream means. At other times, you may need to think on it a bit, so, just as with any other type of dream work, be sure to have the materials ready to write things down. Sometimes you'll need to let the dream sit a bit before it springs into focus.

Some people find that dream programming works almost immediately for them. Others find that it takes longer (depending on things such as how deeply you sleep, how receptive you are to your own suggestions, how much your sleep buddy hits you with that pillow, etc.). In the end, though, if you keep doing it, you'll find that your dreams give you better access to your creative side.

Before discovering this technique, I was a rather left-brained writer; I liked outlines and plotting my story out before I began writing. Once I started dream programming, I found characters, plot twists and entire story lines popping up spontaneously out of the never-never as I needed them.

And it can work this way for you, too.

Whether its painting or acting or writing or thinking outside of the box in your daily life, dream programming can give you access to creative abilities that may have previously been hidden from you. You can use it for the creative arts, but you can also use it to bring creative thinking into every corner of your life, which makes it a pretty useful tool overall.

So sleep deep. Dream big. And then wake up with the answers you need to make your life a more creative and better one.

The End-
And The Beginning

Remembering your dreams. Knowing what kinds of dreams they are. Interpreting your dreams. Programming your dreams for information or insight or creativity. Meeting spirits in your dreams.

We've been on a long road together, and we've covered a lot of territory on our way through the dreamlands. Now it's time to say good bye for now- but while this book has come to an end, this is just the beginning of your own journey, if you choose to make it so.

You have the information. You have the tools to work with. And most of all, you have your dreams, and your dreams can help you to access your own psychic self, tap into your inner wisdom, and find the path that is right for your own perfectly unique journey.

I invite you to use the techniques you've learned in this book to strengthen your intuition, and make your own life better. You'll find that they are useful and versatile tools.

And so, fare well.

I wish you joy.

I wish you peace.

But most of all, I wish you the sweetest of dreams.

Dream big and dream well.

Catherine Kane

References and Helpful Tools for Dreamers

APPENDIX I
Brain Waves

In chapters 11-17, I've talked about different kinds of brain waves and how to work with them to program your sleep patterns and dreams to:

- Remember your dreams.
- Clearly understand and be able to interpret your dreams.
- Chose how often you have psychic dreams.
- Chose what kind of information you are willing to receive, so you don't get information that is overwhelming or excessively personal.
- Program your dreams for creativity.

This appendix is a quick check reference to the different brain wave states that you spend time in while sleeping and waking.

Gamma waves (40Hz) fastest brainwave frequency. Associated with peak concentration, highest state of focus possible, and optimal frequency for cognitive functioning.

Beta waves (13 - 40 Hz) Optimal level for everyday functioning. Alert, wide awake. Mind sharp and focused, making it easier to make connections quickly and easily, helping you achieve peak performance. Great for inspiration, problem solving and tasks that need your full attention.

Alpha waves (8 - 13 Hz) a pleasant and relaxed state of consciousness. Good for stress reduction, creativity and changing your unconscious programming. One of the primary states reached during meditation. You're usually experiencing Alpha waves during REM sleep, which is when you dream the most.

Theta waves (4 - 8 Hz) twilight state between sleeping and waking. Normally experienced while waking or dropping into sleep, but can also be reached through meditation. Also good for relaxation, stress reduction and for reprogramming unconscious beliefs

Delta waves (0 – 4 Hz) Deepest level of sleep and vital for health and well-being.

Studies find that once you fall asleep, you cycle up and down through the delta, theta and alpha throughout the time that you are sleeping. They find that a majority of dreams happen during REM sleep, while you're in Alpha, but that dreaming can occur during any state while you are asleep.

Appendix II –
Glossary

Alim – A Muslim scholar.

Asclepieions - Greek temples devoted to curing illness through dreams .

Brain waves (alpha) – (8-13 Hz) Brainwaves for a pleasant and relaxed state of consciousness.

Brain waves (beta) – (13- 40 Hz) Brainwaves for optimal level for everyday function.

Brain waves (delta) – (0- 4 Hz) Brainwaves for Deepest level of sleep, necessary for health and well-being.

Brain waves (gamma) – (40 Hz) Brainwaves for an optimal frequency for cognitive functioning.

Brain waves (theta) - (4-8 Hz) Brainwaves for the twilight state between sleeping and waking.

Cosm - World: universe.

Dream buddy - A partner to support you in interpreting and working with your dreams.

Dream interpretation - The process of finding the message carried by your dreams.

Dream programming - The process of consciously directing your dreaming for creativity, insight and other useful purposes.

Dream symbols - Dream elements, especially those that have a consistent meaning in your personal dreams.

Dream work- Dream interpretation, dream programming, and other useful ways to work with your dreams.

Element - A part of a dream, whether a person, action, item or other thing. Some elements in a dream are significant and others are not.

Empath - A type of psychic that tunes into emotional vibrations.

The "Five More Minutes" technique - A method for returning to a partially finished dream in order to gain more information or achieve other goals.

Free will - The ability to choose the direction you wish your life to go in.

The Magic Questions - Two simple but very effective questions for accessing the true meaning of your dreams. The Magic Questions are *"What is this element to me?"* and *"How does this element make me feel?"*

Manifestation work – Energy work used to change the nature of reality by attracting or creating things `using non-physical means.

Metaphysics – Any of a wide assortment of non-physical ways of gathering information or working with energy to make things happen.

Mind, conscious – The thoughts and beliefs we have that we are aware of.

Mind, unconscious - The thoughts and beliefs we have that we are not aware of, but that nonetheless have an effect on how we live and what kind of world we create around us.

Oneirocritica - A Roman book on dreaming believed to be both the most famous and most comprehensive volume on the subject in the ancient world. Otherwise known as *The Interpretation of Dreams.*

Oracle - A priest or priestess who delivers prophecies at a shrine dedicated to the consultation of a prophetic god or goddess.

Psychic - 1) Of or pertaining to extraordinary mental processes, especially extrasensory or non-physical ones. Some examples are extrasensory perception or mental telepathy.

2) Receiving information through sources other than the five senses.

3) Person who uses psychic abilities.

Psychic dream - Dream communicating information received through psychic abilities.

Psychic dream, literal – A psychic dream of something that has happened, is happening, or will happen in the future. Information in the dream is received by non physical means.

Psychic dream, symbolic – A psychic dream where the elements of the dream stand for other things.

R.E.M. - Rapid eye movement, the stage during sleep when dreaming occurs.

Scrying - Accessing information psychically by focusing your gaze in a reflective surface, such as a mirror or crystal ball.

Self-hypnosis - A self-induced process of using self suggestion during an altered state to change beliefs and behaviors.

"Setting an intent" – A metaphysical term for setting a goal during dream work, energy work, or manifestation to determine what will happen.

the Sleeping Prophet - Edgar Cayce, one of the most famous and prolific psychics in American history.

Appendix III
Your Personal Dream Symbols

As we discussed in the body of this book, each of us will have a different and unique set of symbols in our own dreams. Many times, a symbol may mean something in one dream and something different in another (a dream of a cuddly cat is different from a dream of a hissing and clawing cat), which is why it's important to look at dream elements in the context of the specific dream.

At the same time, though, most of us will develop some dream symbols that consistently mean one thing for us as individuals, and knowing our own specific personal symbols can help us to be better at getting the most meaning out of our dreams.

Notice something that keeps turning up in dream after dream, and that always seems to mean the same thing? This may be one of your own special symbols. Write it down in this section, and when you've got a handle on it, write down what it means to you.

APPENDIX IV
Dream Journal

This section is for writing down and interpreting your dreams. I've included enough pages for a week of dream recording so that you have enough to get started out with, but if you intend to do this on a long term basis, I'd recommend that you either:

- rip out one sample set of pages, photo copy them and put them into a ring binder.

  or else

- get yourself a notebook specifically for dream interpretation and copy the prompts into it by hand.

Once you've been doing this for awhile, it'll begin to come naturally to you and you may not even need to write and highlite to be able to interpret the dreams, but if you're making this part of your personal practice, it's still a good idea to write them down and have a specific place where you do this. Sometimes the things that dreams are telling us about take a little time to materialize, and we may not make the connection if we don't have a record somewhere of the original dream.

Just remember the steps of dream interpretation are:

- Write down everything you remember about the dream.
- Re-read what you wrote down, and mark any things that jump out at you.
- Look at the elements that jumped out at you. Ask yourself the two magic questions *"What is this element to me?"* and *"How did this element make me feel?"*
- Write down those answers, and then re-read them.
- Tell yourself the story that lies behind the original story of the dream.
- And it's a good idea to also keep track of how your dream worked for you in the waking world and write it down.

Did you dream of something that later happened?
Did your dream give you the answer to a question you'd been wrestling with?
Did it give you information that gave you insight when something happened later in the day?

Having a record of how it worked out will help you to become better at interpreting your dreams later on.
That's all you need to do.
Sweet dreams- and happy waking.

Date-
Write Down Everything I Remember About My Dream

_____

_____

_____

_____

_____

_____

_____

_____

_____

_____

_____

_____

_____

_____

_____

_____

_____

_____

_____

_____

_____

_____

_____

_____

_____

_____

_____

_____

_____

_____

_____

_____

_____

_____

_____

_____

_____

_____

_____

_____

<u>Magic Question 2</u>
<u>"How does this element make me feel?"</u>

_____

_____

_____

_____

_____

_____

_____

_____

_____

_____

Look At Your Answers
Tell Yourself the Story That Lies Behind the Dream

How Did Your Dream Help You In the Waking World?

_____
_____
_____
_____
_____
_____
_____
_____
_____
_____
_____
_____
_____
_____
_____
_____
_____
_____
_____
_____
_____
_____
_____
_____
_____
_____
_____

Date-
Write Down Everything I Remember About My Dream

_____

_____

_____

_____

_____

_____

_____

_____

_____

_____

_____

_____

_____

_____

_____

_____

_____

_____

_____

_____

_____

_____

_____

_____

_____

_____

_____

_____

_____

_____

_____

_____

_____

_____

_____

_____

_____

_____

_____

_____

__Magic Question 2__
__"How does this element make me feel?"__

_____

_____

_____

_____

_____

_____

_____

_____

_____

_____

Look At Your Answers
Tell Yourself the Story That Lies Behind the Dream

_____

_____

_____

_____

_____

_____

_____

_____

_____

_____

_____

_____

_____

_____

_____

_____

_____

_____

_____

_____

_____

_____

_____

_____

_____

_____

How Did Your Dream Help You In the Waking World?

_____

_____

_____

_____

_____

_____

_____

_____

_____

_____

_____

_____

_____

_____

_____

_____

_____

_____

_____

_____

_____

_____

_____

_____

_____

<u>**Date-**</u>
<u>**Write Down Everything I Remember About My Dream**</u>

_____

_____

_____

_____

_____

_____

_____

_____

_____

_____

_____

_____

_____

_____

_____

_____

_____

_____

_____

_____

_____

_____

_____

_____

Re-Read- Mark Every Element That Jumps Out At Me
Magic Question 1 "What is this element to me?"

_____

_____

_____

_____

_____

_____

_____

_____

_____

_____

_____

Magic Question 2
"How does this element make me feel?"

_____

_____

_____

_____

_____

_____

_____

_____

Look At Your Answers
Tell Yourself the Story That Lies Behind the Dream

_____

_____

_____

_____

_____

_____

_____

_____

_____

_____

_____

_____

_____

_____

_____

_____

_____

_____

_____

_____

_____

_____

_____

_____

How Did Your Dream Help You In the Waking World?

_____

_____

_____

_____

_____

_____

_____

_____

_____

_____

_____

_____

_____

_____

_____

_____

_____

_____

_____

_____

_____

_____

_____

_____

_____

_____

_____

_____

_____

Date-
Write Down Everything I Remember About My Dream

Re-Read- Mark Every Element That Jumps Out At Me
Magic Question 1 "What is this element to me?"

_____

_____

_____

_____

_____

_____

_____

_____

_____

_____

_____

_____

Magic Question 2
"How does this element make me feel?"

_____

_____

_____

_____

_____

_____

_____

_____

_____

_____

Look At Your Answers
Tell Yourself the Story That Lies Behind the Dream

_____

_____
_____
_____
_____
_____
_____
_____
_____
_____
_____
_____
_____
_____
_____
_____
_____
_____
_____
_____
_____
_____
_____
_____
_____
_____
_____
_____
_____
_____

How Did Your Dream Help You In the Waking World?

_____
_____
_____
_____
_____
_____
_____
_____
_____
_____
_____
_____
_____
_____
_____
_____
_____
_____
_____
_____
_____
_____
_____

Date-
Write Down Everything I Remember About My Dream

_____

_____

_____

_____

_____

_____

_____

_____

_____

_____

_____

_____

_____

_____

_____

_____

_____

_____

_____

_____

_____

_____

_____

_____

Re-Read- Mark Every Element That Jumps Out At Me
Magic Question 1 "What is this element to me?"

_____

_____

_____

_____

_____

_____

_____

_____

_____

_____

_____

_____

Magic Question 2
"How does this element make me feel?"

_____

_____

_____

_____

_____

_____

_____

_____

_____

_____

Look At Your Answers
Tell Yourself the Story That Lies Behind the Dream

_____

_____

_____

_____

_____

_____

_____

_____

_____

_____

_____

_____

_____

_____

_____

_____

_____

_____

_____

_____

_____

_____

_____

_____

_____

How Did Your Dream Help You In the Waking World?

_____

_____

_____

_____

_____

_____

_____

_____

_____

_____

_____

_____

_____

_____

_____

_____

_____

_____

_____

_____

_____

_____

_____

_____

_____

_____

_____

Date-
Write Down Everything I Remember About My Dream

_____

_____

_____

_____

_____

_____

_____

_____

_____

_____

_____

_____

_____

_____

_____

_____

_____

_____

_____

_____

_____

_____

_____

_____

_____

_____

_____

_____

Re-Read- Mark Every Element That Jumps Out At Me
Magic Question 1 "What is this element to me?"

_____

_____

_____

_____

_____

_____

_____

_____

_____

_____

_____

_____

Magic Question 2
"How does this element make me feel?"

_____

_____

_____

_____

_____

_____

_____

_____

_____

_____

Look At Your Answers
Tell Yourself the Story That Lies Behind the Dream

How Did Your Dream Help You In the Waking World?

_____

_____

_____

_____

_____

_____

_____

_____

_____

_____

_____

_____

_____

_____

_____

_____

_____

_____

_____

_____

_____

_____

_____

_____

_____

_____

<u>Date-</u>
<u>Write Down Everything I Remember About My Dream</u>

Re-Read- Mark Every Element That Jumps Out At Me
Magic Question 1 "What is this element to me?"

_____

_____

_____

_____

_____

_____

_____

_____

_____

_____

_____

_____

Magic Question 2
"How does this element make me feel?"

_____

_____

_____

_____

_____

_____

_____

_____

_____

_____

Look At Your Answers
Tell Yourself the Story That Lies Behind the Dream

_____

_____

_____

_____

_____

_____

_____

_____

_____

_____

_____

_____

_____

_____

_____

_____

_____

_____

_____

_____

_____

_____

_____

_____

_____

_____

_____

How Did Your Dream Help You In the Waking World?

_____

_____

_____

_____

_____

_____

_____

_____

_____

_____

_____

_____

_____

_____

_____

_____

_____

_____

_____

_____

_____

_____

_____

_____

_____

_____

Index

Who is Catherine Kane?

Catherine Kane is a professional psychic, bard, Reiki master, story teller, Christian mystic, teacher, speaker, enthusiastic student of the Universe, maker of very bad puns and overachiever (amongst other things…)

Her life mission is to help people find and live their best and brightest dreams, and she feels that working with your dreams is a great way to start doing that.

She has written four other books so far – "Adventures in Palmistry", "The Practical Empath- Surviving and Thriving as a Psychic Empath", "Manifesting Something Better- Easy, Quick and Fun Ways of Manifesting the Life of Your Dreams", and "The Lands That Lie Between" (an urban fantasy novel.) The odds are good that she'll continue to carry on in this fashion.

Visit Catherine at
www.CatherineKaneWrites.wordpress.com
and as Catherine Kane Writes on Facebook

Catherine can also be found with her husband Starwolf as Foresight at
www.ForesightYourPsychic.com,
www.ForesightYourCTPsychic.wordpress.com
or as Foresight on Facebook.

Also by Catherine Kane

Adventures in Palmistry

Your Destiny is in your hands – and you can have a hand in your destiny! Reading palms can empower and enlighten you, giving you the information you need for the adventure of life, and enabling you to help others around you. And it can be a lot of fun, as well. "Adventures in Palmistry" makes palmistry easy and fun. It will put the power of palmistry in your hands.

Manifesting Something Better: Easy, Quick and Fun Ways to Manifest the Life of Your Dreams

We are always manifesting- so why don't we manifest something better? The world is made of energy, and our own energy determines the things, people and experiences in our lives. Better energy- better life. The trick is to know how to use your energy to manifest the life you want.

This book is here to tell you how to do just that. It's full of simple methods for improving your energy and working with it to manifest the things you want in your life. Easy, fun and practical.

Are you manifesting something better? This book will show you how.

The Practical Empath-
Surviving and Thriving as a Psychic
Empath

Do other people say you're too sensitive? Do other people's emotions overwhelm you? Do you carry abdominal weight you can't seem to lose?

You may be a psychic empath, tuned into emotional energy which can empower or drain you. To use that gift to help yourself and others, you need to learn skills that put you in control of your gift.

This is the book to help you do just that…

The Lands That Lie Between-
An Urban Fantasy with Morgan and Sam

The day that Morgan lost her job, she knew that change was coming. She broke her lease, threw everything she valued in life, including her cat Sam, in her van, kissed her adoptive family goodbye, and started a cross country trek.

She knew change was coming. She expected that.

What she wasn't expecting was elves, or magic walking in the world around her, or the beauty and the danger of the Lands that Lie Between…

**For more information on these books,
please visit Foresight Publications
at <ins>www.ForesightYourPsychic.com</ins>**